How To Survive Bad Bosses

by

Carmen DiNino
Gayle Lanier
Cynthia Stone

Published By:
BRIGHT BOOKS
P.O. BOX 50335
Austin, Texas 78763-0335
512-499-4164   Fax 512-477-9975

Library of Congress Catalog Number   96-84789
ISBN   1-880092-38-7

First Edition

10 9 8 7 6 5 4 3 2

For two extraordinary bosses
DR. MARY LOU CLAYTON and C. W. STEWART,
who have each positively influenced and
enriched my life beyond belief;
and to my son HARRISON
for his cheerful support of his mom's
writing projects

For all my dedicated working FRIENDS
who have survived bad bosses

For GERALD, a great boss,
and for JORDAN, who someday will be one

CONTENTS

Introduction

HOW TO SURVIVE BAD BOSSES

You've had at least one bad boss. Maybe you have one right now! You are not alone. We have all had one, or more. Some people have had *nothing but* bad bosses.

You have to survive in the workplace, even while working under a tyrant, a thief, a liar, an alcoholic, a jackass, you name it! Should you cut your losses and get out? Fight back? Can you do a better job of coping on the job? Can anything good come out of your "bad boss" experience?

This book is a collection of true stories from "bad boss" survivors. Some stayed until they were fired; others quit when they couldn't take it anymore; most took their battle scars with them to the next job. All wanted to make a better choice the next time.

It helps to remember that every workplace is a system. There's something wrong within the system if employees respond with fear, anxiety, and distress.

This book can be your wake-up call to your own situation. What kind of boss do you face every work day? Does his/her management style include:

1. **conflict** – arguments, hostility, criticism, verbal abuse, anger, obsessive-compulsive behavior

2. **distancing** – silent treatment, ignoring employees, withdrawal from interaction, denial, addictive behaviors, closed doors

3. **intimidation** – one up (boss)/one down (employee), compulsive, always right/never wrong, win/lose, never win/win, double bind (damned if I do, damned if I don't)

4. **projection** – blames others for problems, scapegoating, over focuses on a single employee, biased, holds grudges

Try this. Give your boss points on a scale of 1 to 10 if he/she fits into any of the above four categories. If he/she scores less than 10 total points in all categories, count your blessings and give this book to a co-worker in another department. Between 11 and 25 points, be on your guard and update your résumé. More than 25 points, you have some options:

1. remain in denial
2. go home and kick the dog every night
3. complain to everyone you know until they cringe when they see you coming
4. wallow in your misery while hoping your boss will change
5. try some new coping techniques (see below)
6. run, don't walk, to the nearest headhunter and give them your résumé

While you're waiting to interview for a new job (we hope you don't have to wait forever), try these thoughtful strategies:

▶ **Realize that the only behavior that has a chance of changing is yours.**

▶ **Try to communicate with your boss using "I" statements:** "I feel pressured and uncomfortable when you log in my visits to the water fountain."

▶ **Offer solutions:** "I'll try to train my thirst buds to a regular schedule."

▶ **Put a new twist on what the boss just said:** "You're right, upper management should appreciate your attention to detail. Please tell me how many minutes I am allowed at the water fountain."

▶ **Set appropriate limits:** "I would love to discuss the water fountain schedule with you, but I tend to hear people better when they aren't yelling at me."

- ▶ **Stay a little more mature and a little less anxious than your boss:** "I believe you'll find a 2-minute limit at the water fountain will be frustrating to you and to the employees because enforcing it would be unpleasant and possibly illegal. Let's try to come up with something more workable."

- ▶ **Decline to engage in conflict:** "I can't talk to you now. Until you calm down, I'll be at the water fountain."

- ▶ **Stay out of triangles:** "If Howard's water fountain visits are a problem for you, please feel free to speak with him directly. I don't have a problem with him."

or...

- ▶ **You could tell your boss where to stick it:** "Take this $&%&#&^% water fountain schedule and shove it!" ... but be prepared to file for unemployment before the sun goes down. The other strategies have less risk, even if they aren't as much fun!

Good luck!

No matter how bad your boss is, something good can come of it. By examining your work situation, and in the process, learning how *not* to treat others, you have an opportunity to get the rest of your life in balance. As the authors did, you can achieve some personal growth by working on any of the following:

▶ **Get more exercise.**

▶ **Save more money than you did last year.**

▶ **Improve your nutrition.**

▶ **Stay in touch with close friends.**

- ▸ Find a spiritual basis for meaning and purpose in your life.

- ▸ Stop to smell the roses with your family.

- ▸ Learn something new.

- ▸ Take a few risks and persevere undaunted by criticism.

- ▸ Use your God-given talents to touch the hearts of others.

"The fastest way to succeed is to look as if you're playing by the other people's rules, while quietly playing by your own." - MICHAEL KORDA

•••

How to Survive
Bad Bosses

[1]   In my first job as a school principal, I was assigned to a school in the lower income section of town. The man I replaced had already left for his new job, obviously in a hurry, because he forgot to take his liquor bottles with him.

The custodian was immediately hostile to me, and it took some investigating before I discovered that he was drinking partners with the former principal. His boss would get so drunk on a regular basis that the custodian was actually running the school!

There were no financial records, no books kept, but in 10 years no one in administration had noticed. In fact, I was shocked to hear that the former principal left, not because he was fired, but because he was promoted to upper management in the school district!

"Those who can - do. Those who cannot - teach."
- H.L. MENCKEN

"Those who cannot teach - administrate!"
- MURPHY'S LAW

•••

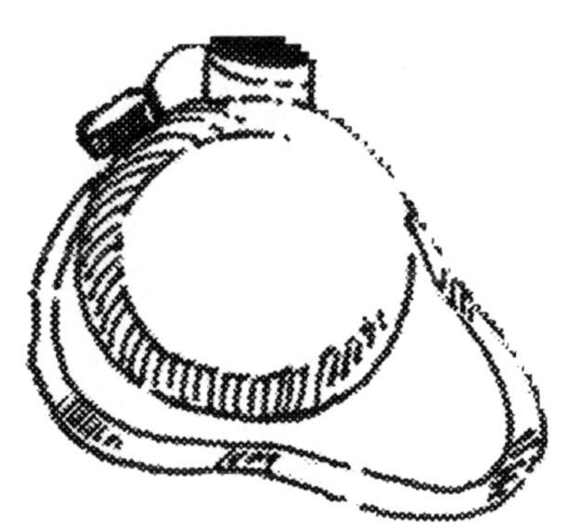

[2]   My boss had been previously convicted of embezzlement, when he was hired to run the finance department of a major government agency. Also an alcoholic supposedly in recovery, he continued to misappropriate funds while at the government agency.

This "former" felon did not object when departmental directors, who were also "recovering" alcohol and drug addicts, purchased art collections, took trips with their secretaries to Acapulco, and gave themselves $100,000 bonuses.

When the government auditors finally reviewed the financial records, he was forced to resign and the agency went into receivership. He was hired immediately in the private sector.

"It is error alone which needs the support of government. Truth can stand by itself."
- THOMAS JEFFERSON

"I am not a crook." *- RICHARD NIXON*

"If I've got a future, it's in government, and when the big man tells me to do something, either I do it for him or he gets someone else who can."
- G. GORDON LIDDY

•••

[3]   I worked for several years as an assistant to the executive director of a federal commission dealing with alcohol and drug abuse issues. During a routine audit, it was discovered that the director had purchased bogus biofeedback equipment for research on addictions, in addition to other unethical practices for which he was eventually forced to resign.

When I was questioned about his "research," I realized that his research subjects were limited to attractive young female administrative assistants. Further investigation revealed that other employees always heard giggling between long silences from behind his locked office door. I discovered that his research consisted of attaching "electrodes" to various body parts and observing the registrations on the "meter." I never found any written documentation of the results of his "studies."

Today this man is in private practice as a therapist and continues to research biofeedback techniques.

"The difference between men and boys is the price of their toys." - LIBERACE

"Power is the ultimate aphrodisiac."
- HENRY KISSINGER

•••

[4]   As the office administrator for the deputy director of a large company, I frequently watched him climb to the second-story roof at the back of the office building first thing in the morning to observe and document employee arrival times. He even got the assistant directors to hide in trees at the entrance of the building, using binoculars to watch the front parking lot. Those who were even five minutes late received a stinging memo which included a threat to dock their pay.

"The trouble with the rat race is that even if you win you're still a rat!" - LILY TOMLIN

"I've developed a new philosophy. I only dread one day at a time." - CHARLIE BROWN

•••

[5]   During a particularly desperate time in my life, I took a job in a convenience store, working for an Iranian who told me in the initial interview that I would be required to be extra nice to customers and have sex with him on a periodic basis (not all the time, because he was married). He assured me he would pay me extra for each time we had sex.

I lost my job when the store was chained shut by the state comptroller agents for his failure to pay sales tax for the past year. Undaunted, my boss cut the chain off the door and was back in business for another week before they discovered he had re-opened. In retaliation, the agents had the door welded shut, but not before he grabbed all the cash and fled the country.

"I may have many faults, but being wrong isn't one of them." - JIMMY HOFFA

"Hell hath no fury like a businessman scorned."
- MILTON FREEDMAN

[6]   Right out of college, I went to work as a manager trainee for Montgomery Ward. I wanted to make a good impression, so without asking, I just assumed that it was my responsibility to be at work almost 12 hours a day, 6 days a week. This meant that I was working as long as the store was open for business. My boss never bothered to inform me that I might arrange a 40-hour work schedule with other managers. From that point on, things went from bad to worse. No matter how hard I tried, I could not please my boss. I felt terrible about myself and my abilities, and I suffered from a poor self-concept.

Ironically, 25 years later I ran into the man who had been the general manager during the time I had worked there. He informed me that not long after I left, he had had to fire the manager I had worked for. "No one could work for him; he was unreasonable; he had to go."

"The wealth of a country is its working people."
- THEODORE HERZL

"If you wish to know what a man is, put him in authority." - SLAVIC PROVERB

•••

[7]   I was forced to make a career change in my mid-30s when the developer I worked for filed bankruptcy. I felt lucky to land a job through my father's political connections with a government agency. I was placed in an administrative role in the print shop section under a manager whom the division director intended to fire. I was told to sit tight until the print shop manager (who was my immediate boss) could be fired. It was implied that I would be promoted into that position once the dismissal took place.

A few weeks later without notice, the division director who hired me left under duress. I was stranded in a brand new job without an ally. In retaliation for what the print shop manager suspected was going on, I was banished to the production floor, stripped of all responsibilities and totally ignored.

I took this opportunity to learn the printing business and retrain myself in a new field as a print purchaser.

"I am here, but I do not exist here."
- JOSE ORTEGA Y GASSET

"Discontent is the first step in the progress of a man or a nation."
- OSCAR WILDE: <u>A Woman of No Importance</u>

•••

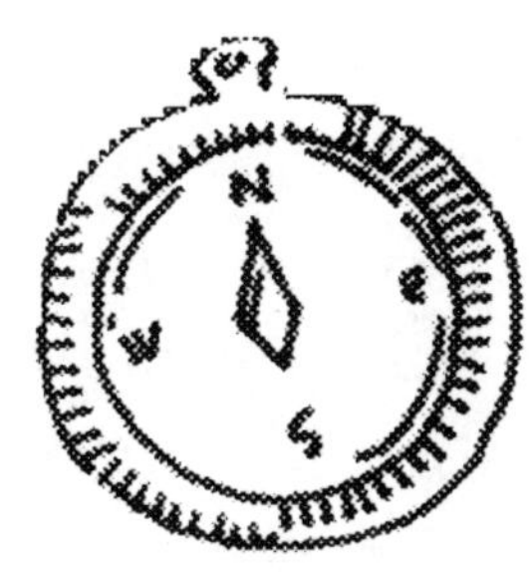

[8] I worked for a short period as a mid-level manager for a highly successful merchant. He was brilliant in marketing and operating his store but seriously lacking in communication skills. When I dared to disagree with him, he would react by yelling profanity or by hurling objects at me from his desk. What made it worse was that he would later apologize for his behavior, appearing genuinely remorseful.

I should have realized when his CPA left after refusing to sign questionable financial documents that my tenure would run short at this company. I stayed until I was told I was being laid off. But it was not until I applied for unemployment benefits and learned of his response to my claim that I knew what he really thought of me. I tried to convince myself that he was saying awful things about me only to escape paying benefits, but I was never sure. Because of that experience, I lost a certain amount of confidence in myself which I have never been able to regain.

"Good breeding consists of concealing how much we think of ourselves and how little we think of the other person." - MARK TWAIN

"The question, 'Who ought to be boss?' is like asking 'Who ought to be the tenor in the quartet?' Obviously, the man who can sing tenor." - HENRY FORD

• • •

[9]   I worked in the savings-and-loan industry in the late 70's at a time when the oil industry was booming and construction start-ups were breaking records every month. I left the large savings-and-loan association where I had received my management training for an opportunity to head up the savings and marketing departments of a small downtown S&L. The president of this association was a unique individual to work for, to say the least. He delighted in talking about his employees behind their backs. At first it seemed innocent enough until I realized that these conversations were anything but innocent.

Soon it became evident that those in the inner circle, who stayed after work and were invited to come in his office to "visit" were the favored few. Those who were not in his favor soon found their offices moved and furniture and other equipment taken away. Social interaction with the president ceased, and the message was sent out that their opinions no longer mattered. If they didn't leave soon after, they would be quietly fired with no explanation given to the staff.

The "in" crowd felt secure and confident about their status until they too fell from grace. We all remained terribly insecure and paranoid, and never knew quite how to behave. For the most part, the staff worked in an isolated fashion, choosing not to develop relationships with each other.

I must admit it was sweet revenge 15 years later to hear of his firing and to know that the federal government was looking into the shady lending practices during his reign of terror.

"Truth is the greatest of all national possessions. A state, a people, a system which suppresses the truth or fears to publish it, deserves to collapse."
- KURT EISNER

"We are afraid of truth, afraid of fortune, afraid of death, and afraid of each other."
- RALPH WALDO EMERSON

•••

[**10**] There was nothing immoral or illegal about the way my boss conducted himself. Two way communication with him was poor; words were difficult from both sides. Maybe I didn't try hard enough, but I never found his heart. I had no choice finally but to leave.

"It is only with the heart that one can see rightly; what is essential is invisible to the eye."
- ANTOINE DE SAINT EXUPÉRY, <u>*The Little Prince*</u>

"Faces we see, hearts we know not."
- SPANISH PROVERB

•••

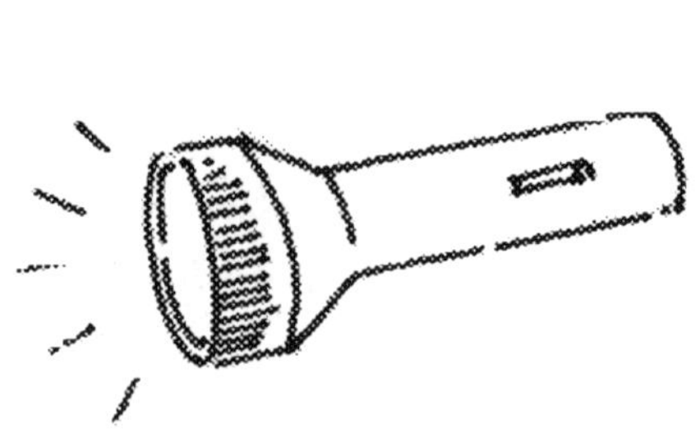

[11] I still remember the Christmas bonus I received one year while working at a retail store. The boss handed out to all employees a bonus of $5, with the taxes withheld. I gave mine back.

"Money is like muck, not good unless it be spread." - FRANCIS BACON

"Render unto Caesar the things that are Caesar's, and unto God what is God's." - MATTHEW 22:21

• • •

[**12**] I remember working as a teacher for a principal who absolutely refused to come out of his office. He was never in the halls, never visited the classrooms, the library, or the cafeteria. This bizarre behavior led to an arrangement among the teachers, who attempted to band together to run the school. Even with their attempt at coordination, classroom control was chaotic. He would promise to help when we confronted him, but we knew he would not follow through. I can't think of one contribution he made while I taught there.

"Men fundamentally can no more get along without direction than they can without eating, drinking, or sleeping." - CHARLES DE GAULLE

"A person may cause evil to others not only by his actions but by his inaction, and in either case he is justly accountable to them for the injury." - JOHN STUART MILL

•••

[13] I had a floor supervisor who never looked at women's faces. He unabashedly stared straight at their chests. I always said that he wouldn't recognize me if I had a mastectomy. He was known as the "chest man."

"I once was lost, but now am found, was blind, but now I see." - JOHN NEWTON, "Amazing Grace"

"Can a blind man lead a blind man?"
- LUKE 6:39

•••

[14] As a psychiatric nurse, I was under constant pressure from attending physicians to exaggerate the symptoms of hospital patients. If patients were not described as needing long-term care, the other nurses and I took much verbal abuse from the doctors who insisted that our observations were understated. We had no recourse in disputing the doctors' claims that we were not "team players." The doctors, on the other hand, could run to the hospital administrator and insist we be fired. Many of us lost our jobs.

"The only thing necessary for the triumph of evil is for good men to do nothing." - EDMUND BURKE

"Those who know the truth are not equal to those who love it." - CONFUCIUS

• • •

[15] One of my early mentors was a young hot-shot CPA who came to the bank where I worked. He was considered brilliant and was quickly elevated to the status of chief financial officer. People marveled at his genius with numbers but trembled from his lack of tact and his explosive nature. His erratic management style was notorious: we never knew whether he was going to throw compliments or verbal grenades in our direction.

When he divorced his first wife, we assumed he had "out grown" her. By the time he was made president, the bank was the fourth largest in the area. Soon after the bust, the bank collapsed, a federal investigation began, and his third wife (younger than the first two) threatened to leave him.

One night he just snapped. He cornered his estranged wife in their home and as the S.W.A.T. team surrounded the house, he fatally shot her in the back rather than surrender. Seconds later, he too was shot and killed by the police. Sad to say, I was not surprised that his life had come unraveled and ended in violence.

"Better a patient man than a warrior, a man who controls his temper than one who takes a city."
- PROVERBS 16:32

"It is hard to fight for one's heart's desire. Whatever it wishes to get, it purchases at the cost of soul." - HERACLITUS

•••

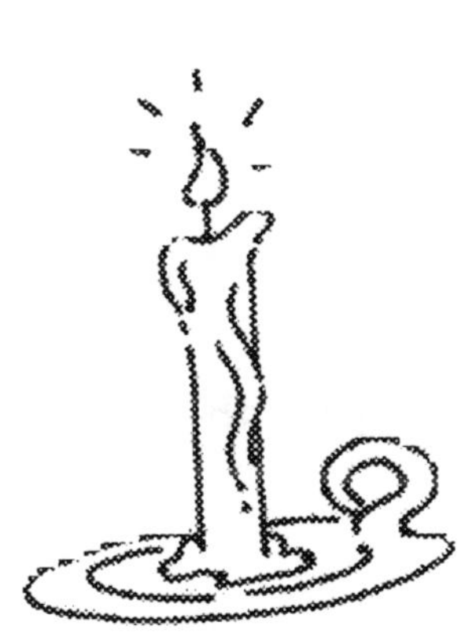

31

[**16**] Compulsive would be a kind word by which to describe my former boss' behavior. Tightwad would be another.

He would get things out of my trash can at night after I had left the office. He'd put little notes on them, asking if I had really meant to throw them away.

All employees would find the used up bottle of Liquid Paper back in their drawers after throwing it away the day before. No matter that it was as dry as the Gobi Desert.

I learned a lot from him: how not to treat people, how to have a heart attack, and how to wad things up — even bottles of Liquid Paper — before I throw them in the trash.

"A man is likely to mind his own business when it is worth minding. When it is not, he takes his mind off his own meaningless affairs by minding other people's business." - ERIC HOFFER

"No amount of genius can overcome a preoccupation with detail." - MURPHY'S LAW

●●●

[**17**] Everyone hated the owner. He was mean and demeaning, stingy, surly, ruthless in his treatment of others, prejudiced, vengeful, manipulative, a real "user." We figured he learned his employee motivation skills while building the bridge over the Kwai River for Colonel Sahito. Slugs would have poured salt on *him!*

He made everyone take a course in CPR from paramedics, who came to the office to hold the classes. He paid for the course, and we could take it after work at night. We decided the only reason he was being so generous about paying for it was because he was paranoid about having a heart attack, and he wanted to be sure that any employee could administer CPR to him in the event he began having chest pains.

What he didn't realize was that no one would have lifted a finger to save him unless he happened to be signing paychecks at the time. Also it never occurred to him that angina in an organ that small would not have caused him much pain.

"When I find my heart, I also find the courage to be myself, for the heart stands for the very self. When I find my heart, I also find the courage to expose myself, for the heart stands for the very point of encounter with self, with others, with God. God sees the heart and only with the eyes of the heart can I see God."
- BROTHER DAVID STEINDL-RAST, <u>*Gratefulness, the Heart of Prayer*</u>

" 'Be yourself' is the worst advice you can give some people."
- MARK TWAIN

• • •

[18] When a co-worker and I quit our jobs after almost five years, our boss never said "Thanks" or "Good Luck" or anything. Not even, "What will you two be doing?" He told the staff and our customers that we were going home to spend more time with our families, since we both had small children. I guess if we had been men, he would have taken a different tack.

I wish I had been a fly on his office wall when he found out customers were transferring their business to our new company.

"If a man rolls a stone, it will roll back on him."
- PROVERBS 26:27

"There's nothing more frightening than igno-rance in action."
- JOHANN WOLFGANG VON GOETHE

•••

[**19**] When I was in college, I got a job in a clothing store near the campus where several of my sorority sisters also worked. We soon got a new manager who really turned us off with all her bragging and lying.

At different times in various conversations, she told us she had gone to law school, medical school, and a girls' college in the East; been a flight attendant, a professional model, and a make-up artist to celebrities. We figured she had to be at least 30 years old to have done all that, not the 23 years on her driver's license.

Her "incredibly dark tan" from the weekend frolicking with hunks by her pool always washed off by Monday; her black eye was from fainting on her balcony; she was being romantically pursued by millionaires; she was thinking of buying a new car — *ad nauseum.*

It was not until I was little older that I realized how inferior she felt around all the sorority girls, who had more than just great looks. For the most part, we had brains, educations and the money to pay for them, and especially social acceptance —

all of which were a ticket out of the place where she would likely be stuck for the rest of her life.

"Lying increases the creative faculties, expands the ego, lessens the friction of social contacts... It is only in lies, wholeheartedly and bravely told, that human nature attains through words and speech the forbearance, the nobility, the romance, the idealism, that — being what it is — it falls so short of in fact and in deed."
- CLARE BOOTHE LUCE

"There are three kinds of lies: lies, damned lies, and statistics." - BENJAMIN DISRAELI

• • •

[20] When I fulfilled requests from my boss, I tried to ignore that some of them were a bit unethical, immoral, or maybe just "not quite right." I didn't realize I was sacrificing my self-respect and my dignity. Gradually, I got angry...angry at myself. I had lost some of my self-love, but I could not pinpoint why I felt so bad about myself. I would wake up each day and just know that something wasn't right.

One day I realized that he wasn't going to fire me for standing up for my principles. Once I overcame that fear, then I built up the courage to quit that job.

"It is easier to stay than get out." - MARK TWAIN

"You gotta know when to fold 'em." from "The Gambler" - sung by KENNY ROGERS

• • •

[**21**] Once I had a Palestinian boss who was the most anti-Semitic person I have ever known. He was convinced that the Holocaust never happened and that the Jews had duped the world into believing in it.

One day he discovered that the office manager he had hired six months ago was Jewish, and within 24 hours he had trumped up a reason to fire one of the most organized, efficient, and effective employees in the whole company.

"We are to decide in favor of civilization or barbarism." - SAM HOUSTON

"If my theory of relativity is proven successful, Germany will claim me as a German and France will declare that I am a citizen of the world. Should my theory prove untrue, France will say that I am a German, and Germany will declare that I am a Jew." - ALBERT EINSTEIN

• • •

[22] Quite a few years ago, when I was in my early twenties, I worked for a group of urologists as a dietitian and assistant. When the office was busy, I would also help schedule appointments.

One day, I scheduled a couple for a consultation and vasectomy (not even knowing what that procedure was at the time) and was surprised to see them leave in a mad hurry within five minutes of their arrival.

The doctor stormed out of his office and demanded to know which of us idiots had set that appointment. When I innocently admitted I had done it, he gruffly called me into his office and berated me for my lack of knowledge. Then he proceeded to inform me that he and the group didn't perform vasectomies because (1) they only did expensive kidney surgeries and vasectomies cost just $150; (2) he was Catholic; and (3) he didn't think it was fair for another man to have such freedom.

"A man's interest in the world around him is only the overflow of his interest in himself."
- GEORGE BERNARD SHAW

"What is freedom? Freedom is the right to choose: the right to create for oneself the alternative of choice. Without the possibility of choice and the exercise of choice, a man is not a man but a member, an instrument, a thing."
- ARCHIBALD MACLEISH

• • •

[23] I worked as an administrative assistant for a state legislator many years ago. He was an alcoholic - rough, tough, and loud. He yelled and cursed so that everyone who worked for him and most of those who knew him were scared to death of him.

He was part of the "Good Ol' Boy" network, and he played the part very skillfully. Many times he called me at home late at night to come pick him and take him home when he was too drunk to drive. I always did.

One morning, I parked in his reserved space, intending to run in and out before he got to work. Before I could move my car, he drove up and stormed inside the Capitol. He grabbed the microphone from the Speaker of the House, who was reading a bill at the time, and screamed, "Some son-of-a-bitch has parked in my parking place, and I bet my goddamn secretary has something to do with it!"

Before I quit working for him, he went to AA. His personality did not change any, but he was sober for the rest of his life.

"Man is the only animal that laughs and has a state legislature." - SAMUEL BUTLER

"The power of man has grown in every sphere, except over himself." - WINSTON CHURCHILL

•••

[**24**] In the summers between college semesters, I worked near my home town for a grain elevator company. The work was physically demanding, and only young strong men were hired. We worked inside rail cars where the temperature often reached 120 degrees. We used probes, six-foot hollow tubes, to test the moisture content of the grain.

Our crew boss was the owner's son. He really enjoyed throwing his weight around, making sure the "boys" knew their place. One of his favorite tricks, when he felt the work was going too slow, was to shut the door of the rail car with the young worker trapped inside.

He did this to me one day. It was suddenly pitch black and red hot. I panicked and yelled, banging on the door until he opened it. I was incredulous that he did it on purpose. When I confronted him about it, he replied, "Well, see that you speed it up if you don't want it to happen again!" I quit on the spot.

"I forgot that every little action of the common day makes or unmakes character, and that therefore what one has done in the secret chamber one has some day to cry aloud on the house-tops."
- OSCAR WILDE

"The moment you grab someone by the lapels, you're lost." - BURT REYNOLDS

• • •

[25] One would think that a military man would have respect for company rules and regulations. Not the vice-president of the restaurant company where I used to manage one of the shops.

He was a heavy drinker and frequently became loud and obnoxious. He took long drinking lunches with his cronies, a bunch of freeloaders who only liked him because he charged all their meals and drinks to the company credit card - entertainment, I suppose. Waitresses were terrified to have him at their station.

One of the company rules was that employees could eat for half-price, but only at the restaurant - no take out, no alcoholic beverages, no family meals included.

On her third day of employment, our new hostess was unlucky enough to take his order for "food to go." She prepared the ticket as she would for any employee: full price. When he saw what she had written on the bill, he pompously demanded to know if she knew who he was. She barely had time to answer in the affirmative before he began to yell at her, accusing her of mistreating customers and being disrespectful to him. It took me 20 minutes to calm her down after he left.

I relished the day he was fired, but it came too late: he had already run off all the smart young managers, including me. Once the news spread of his dismissal, a manager (a retired military crony with no experience in restaurants except as a consumer) ran up a huge bill while boondoggling at company expense at a local hotel and never reported for work again.

"Power does not corrupt man; fools, however, if they get into a position of power, corrupt power."
- GEORGE BERNARD SHAW

"What is man, when you come to think upon him, but a minutely set, ingenious machine for turning, with infinite artfulness, the red wine of Shiraz into urine?"
- ISAK DINESEN, Seven Gothic Tales

[**26**] I learned a great deal from a boss I had many years ago. He was a Harvard MBA, an expert in process and work flow improvement. Soon after I started working at that company, I attended an office party where another co-worker and I accidentally observed my drunken boss strike his girlfriend, also an employee. We were not sure if he knew we saw the incident.

She came to work the next day with stitches and said she slipped in the tub. I am certain I would handle it differently today, but at the time, I said nothing more to her or anyone else about it.

Soon it became obvious to us that he knew we witnessed his abuse of her. Within a week, my boss started making personal attacks on us, verbally and in writing. Later, after a successful season, I got a poor review, but nothing of substance, only style issues. I was laid off six months later in an organizational reshuffle. Within a year, my boss was also fired.

"It is very easy to forgive others their mistakes; it takes more grit to forgive them for having witnessed your own." - JESSAMYN WEST

"There are more pleasant things to do than beat up people." - MUHAMMED ALI *(from one of his retirement speeches)*

•••

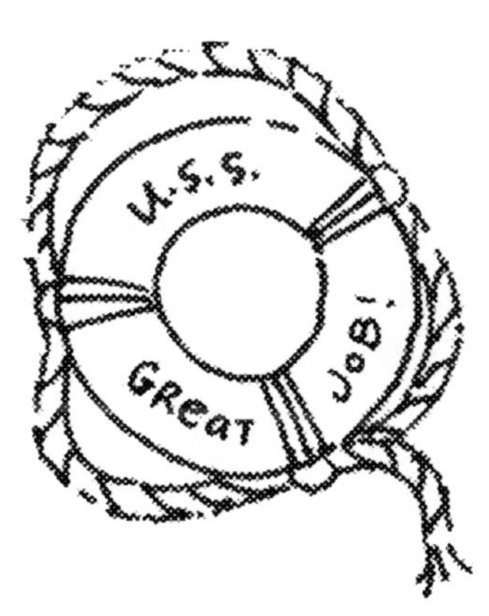

[27] My boss told the employees I managed how much he was paying me. When I complained, he acted as though it were no big deal and said he thought it was common knowledge how much I made.

Three months later, our new employee manual was issued. It contained a section stating that discussion of salaries was grounds for immediate dismissal.

"Justice is justice though it's always delayed and finally done only by mistake."
- GEORGE BERNARD SHAW

"The average man's judgment is so poor, he runs a risk every time he uses it." - E.W. HOWE

• • •

[28] You want to know about anal retentive? I'll show you anal retentive. My boss loved to "high-light" the obvious and the obscure in any number of colors on the same page. Once he sent back my expense report (delaying my reimbursement check), with a 21¢ error highlighted in bright yellow. My mistake was in the company's favor.

"The difference between genius and stupidity is that genius has its limits." - ALBERT EINSTEIN

" 'Shut up!' he explained." - RING LARDNER

• • •

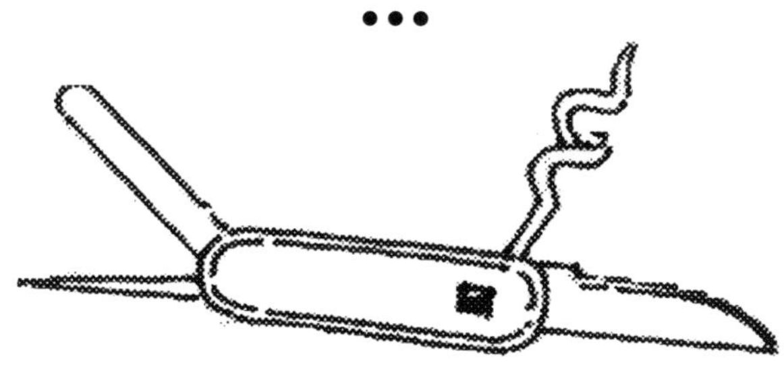

[29] During my senior college year, while a starving newly-wed as well, I worked as assistant bookkeeper for a man who owned a chain of laundries. He had borrowed money from his wife's father to start the business. My office was next to his in the suite upstairs over the floor of the plant.

The couch in his office backed up to the wall behind my desk. When his girlfriend came to visit, he would lock the door, and in about five minutes I could hear the couch rhythmically bumping the wall. That was annoying in itself, but it really bothered me when his wife or his father-in-law called, and I would have to lie to them about his activities or whereabouts.

I guess my vows were too fresh on my mind, so I quit.

"There must be 500,000 rats in the United States;
of course, I am only speaking from memory."
- BILL NYE

"Whoever called it necking was a poor judge of
anatomy." - GROUCHO MARX

•••

[**30**] The high tech industry seems to attract lots of unusual people. My boss was a bisexual transvestite. He made all the women in his department go shopping for women's clothes for him on their lunch hours. I knew eventually it would be my turn.

Unfortunately, he accompanied me on my assigned shopping excursion. We went shopping together, not for dresses, but for wigs! I had to try them on and model for him so he could make a selection.

I guess I would not have minded the favor so much if he had been more effective as a boss and not gotten the women to do his work for him as well.

"Costly thy habit as thy purse can buy,
But not express'd in fancy, rich, not gaudy,
For the apparel oft proclaims the man."
- WILLIAM SHAKESPEARE, <u>Hamlet</u>
(Act I, scene iii - Polonius)

"There is no such thing as a moral dress...it's people who are moral or immoral."
- JENNIE JEROME CHURCHILL

•••

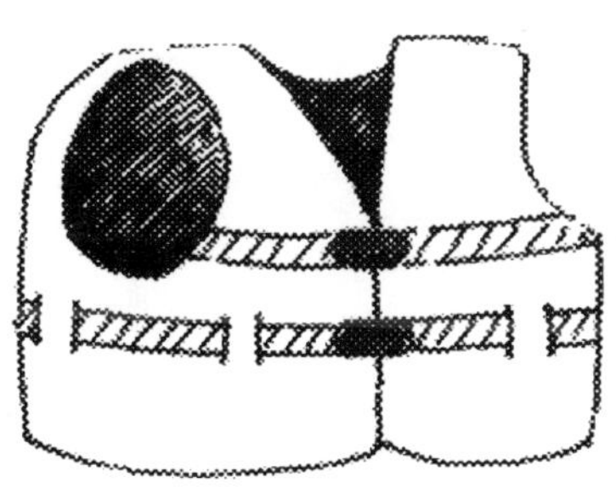

[31] The only thing I hate more than liars are cheats, and my boss was both! He was a perfectionist who could never meet deadlines because he changed his mind so much. Then he would blame me, and I would have to work overtime to complete his project. He told me I could not be compensated for my extra hours because I was "non-exempt."

When I transferred to another division, I found out I was eligible after all, so I sued for back compensation and won!

"Corn can't expect justice from a court composed of chickens." - AFRICAN PROVERB

"In passing, also, I would like to say that the first time Adam had a chance, he laid the blame on woman..." - NANCY ASTOR

•••

[32] Looking back on my interview, I can't believe I actually said, "I will not sleep with any boss!" I am glad I had the nerve to say it to this boss in particular.

It was not long before I discovered he was an alcoholic and a drug user, who also dealt in pornography. He was fuzzy-brained much of the time, but that did not keep him from making constant sexual innuendoes in almost every conversation with all the women who worked for him. He had X-rated cards in his Rolodex, and frequently he left some pornographic program running on his computer screen, then he would call one of us in his office for some ridiculous reason just to see how we would react.

One day he handed me a packet of photos to "check for errors in processing." I thought they were probably something for a client, but I was shocked to discover they were photos of a sex orgy. I quit my job because I was afraid of him.

I heard later he left the country because the IRS and the state were after him for back taxes.

"Income tax has made more liars out of the American people than golf has." - WILL ROGERS

"Everything wrong seems possible today, and is accepted. I don't accept it." - PABLO CASALS

•••

[33] Don't believe that fraternity brothers are friends for life! I work for some of mine in the building industry. These guys have so much money that they travel and hunt most of the year just to keep themselves busy. They are hopelessly out of touch with how the work force lives. When they visit the office, they make life hell for everyone.

Our office secretary had been with the company for over ten years, and they paid her just $1,200 a month. She was a little older, plain, reliable and conscientious, but not good enough by their standards. Rather than send her for computer training, they wanted me to fire her and hire someone more "up-to-date." Reluctantly, I did what they wanted.

Within six months, they had hired and fired several secretaries, including a transvestite and a beauty queen who rarely showed up for work.

*"I won't be old till my feet hurt,
and they only hurt when I don't let 'em dance
enough, so I'll keep right on dancing."*
- BILL "BOJANGLES" ROBINSON

*"Women deserve to have more than twelve years
between the ages of twenty-eight and forty."*
- JAMES THURBER

• • •

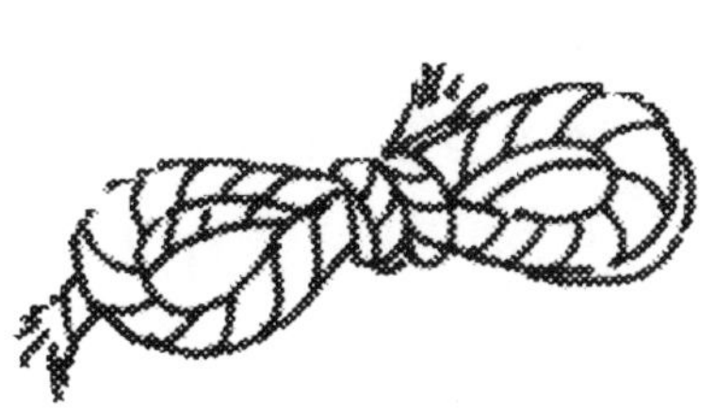

[34] Our school was chaos, thanks to the principal and the kindergarten teacher who ran it. When I first started teaching there, my lessons were cast aside so often with sudden orders to bring the children to the playground for special events day or to assemble them in the cafeteria for art all day that I gave up making lesson plans. I could not get enough continuity of schedule to complete a unit of study. The kids were actually learning and retaining very little.

The other teachers never could figure out whom those two were trying to impress. They drove me out of teaching. I quit and went to law school instead.

"O blessed conceit, where would we be without you?" - RUDYARD KIPLING

"Education is the ability to listen to almost anything without losing your temper or your self-confidence." - ROBERT FROST

•••

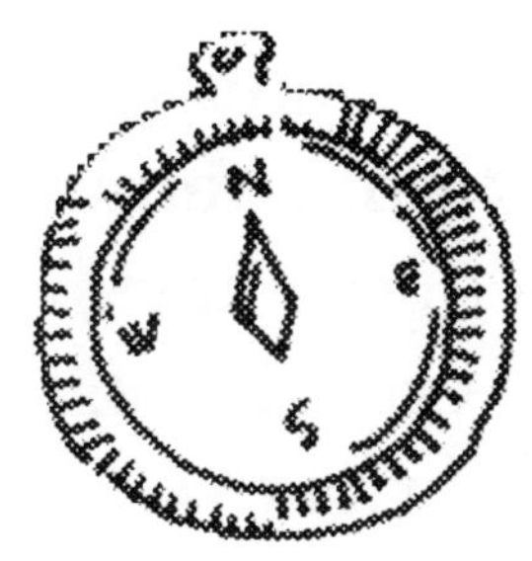

[35] Numbers don't lie, but people do! My job was to interpret numbers from raw data collected by branch offices and then to issue statistical reports which would be used to determine company policy. I considered the numbers to be quite important, so I gave them careful scrutiny, as did many others before turning them in.

The problem was the upper management. If they disagreed with the findings, they simply changed the numbers. Never once did they bring in the branch personnel to answer questions. If I raised an objection, they always gave me the same answer: "Those people are incompetent. Their data can't be trusted."

"Get your facts first, and then you can distort them as much as you please." - MARK TWAIN

"Truth is such a rare thing, it is delightful to tell it."
- EMILY DICKINSON

• • •

[36] My boss was good at passing tests, but that was about it. That's how she got her job as a manager of the government agency where I worked a few years ago. She simply passed a test.

The rest of us worker bees knew she had not a clue about what we did and could not have helped us in a crisis if someone had held a gun to her head.

She asked us to work overtime frequently because she mismanaged so many projects. When we would ask her for a raise, she would always say, "Sure, okay, I'll see what I can do." No one in our division, in the three years I was there, ever got a raise.

"*I am working for the time when unqualified blacks, browns and women join the unqualified men in running our government.*"
- SISSY FARENTHOLD

"*I don't make jokes. I just watch the govern-ment and report the facts.*" - WILL ROGERS

•••

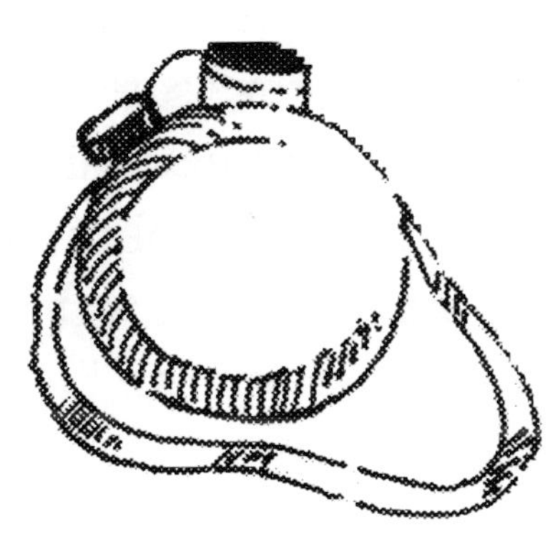

[37] If I knew then what I know today about sexual harassment in the workplace, I probably would not have put up with the middle-aged pervert who was vice president of finance. He periodically reviewed the books and inventory with certain of us office girls, all young and attractive. Just out of college, I worked for a major clothing manufacturer as an office administrator.

We knew what figures he was really going to review after the first five minutes. He spent the rest of the time asking personal questions about our "social" lives. Then he would say things like, "That's a gorgeous blouse! Too bad it's not cut lower!" or "That looks nice on you. Now turn around, let me see it from the back... again, only slower this time."

We endured his off-color comments and innuendoes. I refused to blush and was proud that I could shock him with a few rebuttals of my own. Eventually I was promoted out of the office. I like to think it was because he felt threatened by me.

"A mode of conduct, a standard of courage, discipline, fortitude, and integrity can do a great deal to make a woman beautiful." - JACQUELINE BISSET

"I don't want any yes-men around me. I want everybody to tell me the truth even if it costs them their jobs."
- SAMUEL GOLDWYN

•••

[38] A promotion is not always good news. I moved from administration to production, working directly for the owner of the company. He bullied everyone, from the front line to the senior staff. He was thoroughly macho and not the least bit inhibited about showing it. He belittled employees, screaming at the top of his lungs, assigning blame to the nearest scapegoat. He was notorious for exploding and leaving the injured person to "just fix it!"

I derived some satisfaction from knowing that if I could work for this guy, I could work for anyone.

"Few people can be happy unless they hate some other person, nation or creed."
- BERTRAND RUSSELL

"People who fly into a rage always make a bad landing." - WILL ROGERS

• • •

[39] Growing companies can be dangerous for your health. I worked for a small high tech manufacturer which was rapidly gaining a competitive market share. At the time I was hired, the staff was increasing by about 20 people per week, all hired by the acting marketing director.

When I met the newly-hired vice president of marketing, I could not believe how bad his manners were. Further contact with him convinced me he had been abused as a child. He was simply the meanest, nastiest, most destructive person I have ever met. He was especially gleeful if he could humiliate someone in front of co-workers in the most sarcastic way imaginable. Many of the employees would leave his office near tears. One design engineer shoved a machine at him and then stomped out.

People were trying to get their former jobs back as fast as they could. I felt sorry for the ones who had sold their homes and uprooted their families to move across the country.

One co-worker, a Vietnam veteran with a hilariously dark sense of humor, offered to kill the guy. It was tempting, and I'm sure he wasn't the only one who wished someone would pull a trigger. I don't know how the v-p made it to his car alive at night.

He hired his buddies from his former place of employment, some of whom were put into positions where they had very little experience. The owner was young, so I guess he didn't know any better.

Within 3 months, most of the people the acting marketing director had hired were laid off, including me and another poor soul whose teenager had died a few weeks earlier. I was sorry to be out of a job, but not *that* job.

It gave me perverse satisfaction to learn a few months later that the CEO took this wretch to a rehab hospital in another state for his drug and alcohol abuse problem. Soon an announcement was made that he would not be returning to work. His buddies were quickly laid off in their turn, here one day, gone the next. I wonder if any of them learned anything from this experience.

"The only thing we learn from history is that we do not learn." - EARL WARREN

"I resent large corporations. They flatten personalities." - BOB NEWHART

• • •

[40] *Caveat emptor!* Buyer beware! I could not sleep at night if I had cheated a customer the way my boss did. An older widow, whose recently deceased husband had always bought their cars throughout the years, came into the dealership where I worked. She wanted to purchase a new car from one of the owners and told him her budget was a $350 per month payment.

He waltzed her out onto the showroom floor and helped her pick out a new model, just the color she wanted. Then he proceeded to charge her more than the sticker price so the payment would "fit her budget."

"For what shall it profit a man, if he shall gain the whole world, and lose his own soul?"
- MARK 8:36

"Lady...lady, I do not make up things. That is lies. Lies is not true. But the truth could be made up if you know how. And that's the truth."
- LILY TOMLIN, *as Edith Ann*

[41] There was at least once when I know I was a bad boss. I had an employee in my division who was ambitious beyond his skill and experience. He had trouble with spelling and proof reading, and sometimes he argued with me about word usage. He frequently sent things to customers without checking them carefully or even showing them to me, and more than once I had to take the heat for his mistakes, since the projects were ultimately my responsibility.

Finally, I decided to take him out of the loop on major stuff, so I allowed him to be just "traffic manager" and keep inventory and schedules. I robbed him of his sense of "ownership" in the goals, even the tasks. I knew he was bored to death, but I gave up trying to give him constructive feedback; I merely hoped he would quit. I couldn't fire him since the company vice president liked him for kissing up well.

If I had gone to the v-p with my list of mistakes and problems due to this employee, I knew somehow it would turn out to be my fault: either I was difficult to work for because I was too demanding and opinionated; or I was unfair and unreasonable; or I couldn't see things from anyone's point of view but my own.

I was caught between the proverbial rock and the hard place. Damned if I do; damned if I don't. I finally decided the company v-p was at least partly right: I am difficult to work for because I insist on top quality, and I can't see things from any point of view except the customer's, but I don't think that's unfair or unreasonable. I could not battle them both, so I took a similar job with another company where the work ethic and attitude are more in tune with mine. We're all happier now, I'm sure.

"Every normal man must be tempted at times to spit on his hands, hoist the black flag, and begin slitting throats." - H.L. MENCKEN

"I would like to take you seriously, but to do so would affront your intelligence."
- WILLIAM F. BUCKLEY, JR.

• • •

[42] Sometimes you get to be there when the tables are turned. If my former boss had been more in tune with his staff, he might still have his job as a high level official of a resource agency. He was a poor communicator, but he blamed many of his problems on his staff.

Using government equipment, staff and time, he violated a federal law by stampeding big game from one state to another, then firing a net gun to bring the animals back into his home state. He was so busy firing the gun that he ignored the warnings from the ground crews that the helicopter was straying across the state line. He claimed no one warned him.

If his staff had had any respect for him at all, we might have cut him a little slack. His timing was also very poor, since he pulled this stunt at a time when the agency was under intense scrutiny for accusations concerning stocking fish and wildlife on private ranches of politicians. As it was, there was another stampede following his escapade: his employees could not wait to talk to agency officials and the press about his misconduct. He was out of there!

"Suppose you were an idiot and suppose you were a member of Congress. But I repeat myself."
- MARK TWAIN

"The old Lakota was wise. He knew that man's heart away from nature becomes hard; he knew that lack of respect for growing, living things soon led to lack of respect for humans, too."
- CHIEF LUTHER STANDING BEAR

•••

[43] Sometimes we know we are overqualified and we take the job anyway. Then we find out we are even more qualified than our bosses.

I had just graduated from Princeton with a degree in political science when I took an apprentice position in the mayor's office in a big city. I worked for the criminal justice task force; my job was collating hundreds of mailing pieces and preparing my boss for media meetings. I did not mind the menial work; I expected to have to learn the ropes, and I was glad to be involved at any level.

My boss had no experience or qualifications for her job as director of the task force. What she did have, however, was a father who was president of the Chamber of Commerce and five years' experience as a Las Vegas showgirl.

Her training as a dancer did not mean she could choreograph anything. We were a competent team who could have carried each project to completion without her help, but instead of trusting us, she clung to every detail of our repetitive tasks. She unnerved us with her constant interference. The day she followed behind me, checking every envelope I stuffed, I finally quit.

She went on to a higher paying job in the governor's office. She might have managed to keep that job for a long time, but she became pregnant out-of-wedlock and was finally forced to leave.

"The best minds are not in government. If any were, business would hire them away."
- RONALD REAGAN

"Satan fell by the force of gravity: he took himself too seriously." - LORD CHESTERTON

• • •

[44] Most people misinterpreted my boss' behavior as exhibiting confidence, but a few of us knew she was really insecure. She was the type who would go over someone's head for a decision he was authorized to make, just to keep him off balance. Part of her operating style included sending nasty memos to coworkers' superiors about some unfounded problem. She would hold selective staff meetings and openly criticize the actions of other employees, being careful not to include anyone in the meeting who could dispute her word.

I guess she knew I saw through her and she felt threatened by me. She would introduce me as the "person responsible for licensing" instead of by my actual position: company attorney.

"Be humble, for the worst thing in the world is
of the same stuff as you; be confident, for the
stars are of the same stuff as you."
- NICHOLAI VELIMIROVIC

"The brain is a wonderful organ; it starts working the moment you get up in the morning and
does not stop until you get to the office."
- ROBERT FROST

•••

[45] I would never buy a used car from my former boss, or even a new one, and here's why. I worked at a well-known family-owned dealership in sales, and one day my boss, one of the owners, overheard me answering questions from my customer, a school teacher. He interjected helpful information immediately, saying the teacher could get a loan at special rates from the teachers' credit union just by putting the dealership's name on the credit application. She decided to think about it.

After she left, I followed my boss into his office and asked to know more about this special loan program, since it sounded so good. My boss looked at me sympathetically, shook his head and in a condescending tone, said, "Don't be so stupid. There's no such program. Look, if you want to succeed in this business, you've got to learn how to lie."

*"Honesty pays, but it doesn't seem to pay
enough to suit some people."* - KIN HUBBARD

*"Though I am not naturally honest,
I am so sometimes by chance."*
- WILLIAM SHAKESPEARE, <u>The Winter's Tale</u>
(Autolycus, Act IV, scene iv)

•••

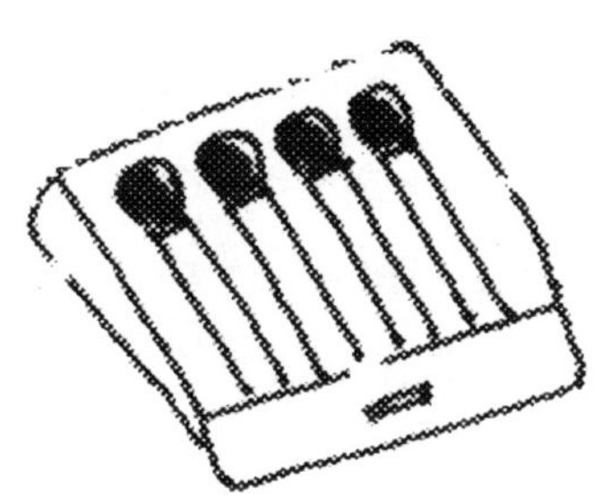

[46] I learned the finer points of bookkeeping from a pair of ministers, a husband and wife team who had enough inherited wealth to make earning a living unnecessary. I kept simple books for the church and complicated ones for them.

The office was always a disaster: papers strewn everywhere, pizza boxes and soft drink cans tossed on the floor, as if they were manna from heaven. I literally carved out a path to get to my desk.

Finally I could take no more of the daily rubbish, and I quit. He asked me to fill out the W-2 and W-3 forms for the IRS before I left. I was very careful to provide him with the originals and file copies, but I mailed my own W-2 to the IRS. Somehow I knew he could not be trusted.

Sure enough, on April 15th of the following year, he sent me a certified letter demanding the payroll information. Included was a copy of what he had written to the IRS: his bookkeeper was at fault because she left without filing the necessary paperwork.

As I mailed my own tax return that day, I was glad I had shaken off the dust from that town and moved on. I was relieved to be rid of that nut!

"I am still determined to be cheerful and happy in whatever situation I may be, for I have also learned from experience that the greater part of our happiness or misery depends on our disposition and not on our circumstances."
- MARTHA WASHINGTON

"A man comes to believe in the end the lies he tells about himself to himself."
- GEORGE BERNARD SHAW

•••

[47] Would you present something out loud to a group when you did not write it yourself, or even know who did write it? My boss, an elusive elected official, made speeches around the state and unknowingly recited words crafted from a variety of sources. The writing started with me, passed through a sacred hierarchy of three supervisors before landing on the desk of the director of media services.

It was hilarious to watch the mad scramble of run-on rewrites, since no one had enough job security to pass on a document without altering it. Many times when a speech reached the final enlightened level, it would merely ricochet off the director's desk and begin a downward spiral until it reached me again, almost unrecognizable.

Just before I left the department to take a new job, I had an opportunity to talk to the commissioner himself. He began to question me about the use of a certain passage in a speech he thought I had written. When I told him I had not written it, he was amazed.

He had no idea how elaborate and rigid the

chain of command was in his own agency. The key to keeping one's job there was to follow the pecking order blindly. I knew there was no way to fight it.

"Well, I would — if they realized that we — again if — if we led them back to that stalemate only because that our retaliatory power, our seconds, or strike at them after our first strike, would be so destructive that they couldn't afford it, that would hold them off." - RONALD REAGAN (asked if nuclear war could be limited to tactical weapons)

"He can compress the most words into the smallest idea of any man I ever met."
- ABRAHAM LINCOLN

•••

[48] Lawrence Welk my boss was not! He was the director of a large university orchestra and band and had replaced a much beloved conductor who was sophisticated and gifted. My boss' experience and credentials looked good on paper, but working for him was disastrous. He treated students and faculty alike as if he were the only competent one, but failed miserably to challenge the limits of our abilities, trying to control us through rigid rules. We were depressed and angry to be stuck with him.

One afternoon, during a football game where the band was to perform, everyone noticed a small twin-engine airplane flying overhead, with a message banner trailing behind it. From the derogatory words about the director, we all knew some of his students were out for revenge! The crowd cheered and laughed, all but him.

Several months later, the students and the faculty got our wish: he was relieved of his conductorship and replaced by someone competent and motivational.

"If you prick us, do we not bleed?
If you tickle us, do we not laugh?
If you poison us, do we not die?
And if you wrong us, shall we not revenge?"
- WILLIAM SHAKESPEARE, <u>The Merchant of Venice</u>
(Act III, scene i, Shylock)

"Some men are born mediocre, some men achieve mediocrity, and some men have mediocrity thrust upon them." - JOSEPH HELLER

•••

[49] Paradise lost is sometimes paradise found! I once worked for the pastor of a large contemporary church. At first I thought I was in heaven because I was very spiritual and had dreamed of having a job where I could do God's work at the office as well as at home. Everything seemed so happy and positive, almost too upbeat.

As time went by, I noticed that things were not quite as spiritual as they seemed. Acquisition of money was the focus of the church work, except on Sundays. All activities were directed toward getting more donations to build a bigger and better church and to pay bigger and better salaries to the pastor and his wife.

I began to feel nauseated by the hypocrisy: what the pastor said on Sunday was not his true agenda during the week. At the office, he made no effort to hide his quest for more money, mistakenly believing the staff supported his philosophy. We were, in fact, horrified.

The worst for me was when he told me to screen his phone calls and appointments and limit them to church members who contributed $20,000 or more per year. He simply refused to see or talk to anyone who gave under that amount, much less the poor widow who gave only a mite.

I decided to quit my job and pray for his soul.

"Avarice is the sphincter of the heart."
- MATTHEW GREEN

"If there is no hell, a good many preachers are obtaining money under false pretenses."
- WILLIAM A. "BILLY" SUNDAY

• • •

[50] I thought I had it made when I went to work for a commercial painting crew. The boss paid well and usually had lots of work for us. Each day I showed up for work, however, I realized everyone but me was consistently stoned. The foreman even purchased beer for the crews. Good pay and free beer! How can you beat that?

After a while, I also realized that I was the only one getting any work done. I had chosen not to drink or smoke pot on the job; I never had before, why start now? The boss had set up a system by which workers would get drunk, they would do poor work, and then he would yell at them and wonder why he could not get decent help these days!

It was just too negative an environment for me, so I quit. It was a really sick system, dysfunctional is what it would be called today.

"I hate to advocate drugs, alcohol, violence or insanity to anyone, but they've always worked for me." - HUNTER S. THOMPSON

"Even though a number of people have tried, no one has yet found a way to drink for a living."
- JEAN KERR

•••

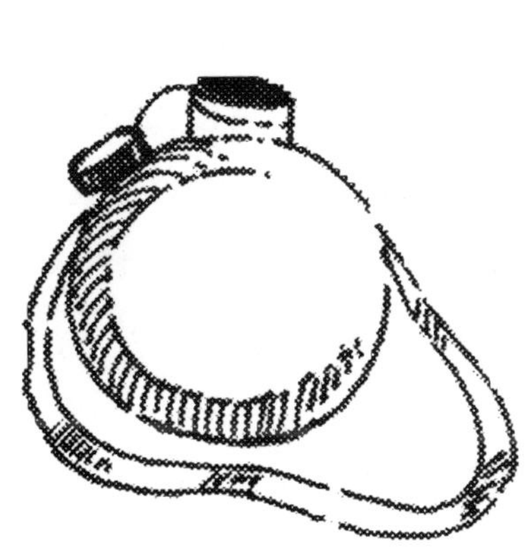

[51] Getting my license as a psychologist was supposed to take two years under the direction of a clinical supervisor who would meet with me once a week to review my case load of clients and give me feedback. After the first 12 months, my boss informed me that none of our sessions would count because he felt that he had not "supervised me properly." Reviewing the supervision manual with him was no help. A whole year down the drain, after years of education and grueling preparation! Terror filled my heart, I was dumbfounded, too numb to speak or argue. I went home and cried myself to sleep.

I awoke with a bright idea: I could receive my licensure from the other therapist who was simultaneously supervising me for a different license. She was certified in both areas. When I got to the office, I thanked my boss for pointing out his inadequacy, told him his services would no longer be needed and I would get my license elsewhere.

A short time later, I heard this supervisor was fired for failure to supervise clients and employees in circumstances similar to mine. Word spread that he had obsessive personality disorder and was impaired beyond help!

"The best index to a person's character is (a) how he treats people who can't do him any good, and (b) how he treats people who can't fight back."
- ABIGAIL VAN BUREN'S "Dear Abby" newspaper column

"I'd like to get to the point where I can be just as mediocre as a man." - JUANITA KREPS

•••

[52] My boss had many remarkable talents. He was a famous, gifted and brilliant musical talent, a director of one of the premiere symphonies in the world. He was also a tyrant, a prima donna, and a manic/depressive. He would get so angry he could not control his cruelty to the professional musicians he directed. He broke batons and threw them at the cellos, yelled at the violins, told the brass section they were stupid, accused the wind instruments of not being able to read music, and said the tympani could not even count to four.

We were brilliant musicians in our own right, but he was also correct in one thing: we were stupid enough to let him treat us that way. We enabled him to harass and bully us.

Eventually he died of a heart attack at a relatively young age. I wish I could remember him for his genius and his music rather than for his atrocious behavior.

*"I'm a very good man. I'm just a very bad wiz-
ard." - FRANK L. BAUM, in <u>The Wizard of Oz</u>
(Wizard to the Tin Man)*

*"No one acknowledges the fiddle after the con-
cert — they only applaud the fiddler.
Acknowledge the fiddle in your life."
- ANONYMOUS*

•••

[53] I'll say one thing for my boss. She never played favorites, she treated everyone the same: really rotten! She talked rudely to staff and customers alike. She got away with ignoring all her work, leaving customers lined up while she enjoyed private phone conversations, always while the owner was out of the office.

The most embarrassing times were when she would call her husband and order him to wash the clothes, clean the house, and have dinner ready when she got home! She would also gossip in a loud critical way, sometimes quite viciously. She was usually irritated because things were never good enough for her. All this awful talk was overheard by customers.

Thankfully, the owner eventually found out about her slack work habits and fired her. It wasn't until she left that we realized the toxic effect one person can have on the workplace. Our office is now a more peaceful and respectful place to work. We feel like we have our dignity back.

"The hardest job a kid faces today is having good manners without seeing any."
- FRED ASTAIRE

"If only her brain worked as well as her jaws!"
- COLLETTE, from <u>Gigi</u>

•••

[54] From the first interview, my boss seemed a little weird to me, but there wasn't anything specific I could put my finger on. Sometimes I felt dirty after he looked at me. I was the receptionist in his office and could keep a certain distance.

He was an influential and prominent psychiatrist in our community. He had numerous female and pediatric clients, who seemed to love him and be afraid of him simultaneously. Rumors arose that he was a bit too close to his clients.

Every now and then, I got phone calls from women that smacked of jealousy. One day, the police arrived at the office and arrested him for sexual misconduct with clients and with minors. He was charged with molesting his clients.

I was sick about the situation. I had ignored my intuition because I had no hard facts. I quit that job.

The really awful part is that he hired slick, high-priced attorneys who got him off. He is still in private practice.

"The Great Spirit, in placing men on the earth,
desired them to take good care of the ground
and to do each other no harm."
- YOUNG CHIEF, Cayuse tribe

"No one is more arrogant toward women, more
aggressive or scornful, than the man who is anxious about his virility."
- SIMONE DE BEAUVOIR, <u>The Second Sex</u>

• • •

[55] Want to stand up and rock the boat? Go ahead! In some places, that's the only way things will change.

I was an assistant to a teacher who could not teach. She assigned her young students busy work, to be supervised by me, while she went out to her fancy car and talked to her boyfriend on her mobile phone. I guess she could manage her own money, but that was about it! She couldn't manage to get lesson plans done or complete a unit on any course of study.

After threats of lawsuits from parents who knew their children were not even learning to read or write in this woman's class, the principal finally encouraged her to transfer to another school, or perhaps another vocation. She moved to a different school to inflict her damaging style on other children. Unfortunately, she has tenure and I suppose the bureaucracy is afraid to fire her.

"Only the mediocre are always at their best."
- JEAN GIRAUDOUX

"Everybody who is incapable of learning has taken to teaching." - OSCAR WILDE

•••

[56] Not all workaholics work! My boss was respected in his field, dedicated, very nice, and worked extra long hours. I thought he closed his office door so he could concentrate better and conduct his department's business over the phone. His rolodex was larger than average, and we all knew that he talked on the phone continuously. What major executive doesn't?

Imagine how naive we felt when he was arrested for making obscene phone calls! Caught by sophisticated technology, he was publicly accused and left his office in disgrace. He eventually got into treatment for this addiction, concurrent with his incarceration.

Now that I think about it, I guess there were signs: his being so secretive, frequently with a look of shame or guilt on his face. I am certainly going to be more suspicious of my bosses from now on. And I hate that.

"Everyone carries around his own monsters."
- ALDOUS HUXLEY

"Erotica is about sexuality, but pornography is about power and sex-as-weapon — in the same way we have come to understand that rape is about violence, and not really about sex at all."
- GLORIA STEINEM

•••

[57] I still fantasize about the possible headlines: "Control Freak Out of Control !" or "Boss Who Calls All the Shots Shoots Self in Foot !"

Not only was my boss an abusive and autocratic executive, he also maintained absolute control of the auditing and reconciliation functions of the accounting department where I worked. He treated us as if we were stupid, incompetent crooks and said we couldn't be trusted to be accurate, when in fact, we were all respected accountants.

We felt vindicated when he was arrested, charged, and convicted of embezzling several million dollars in company funds. Even then his control freak behavior didn't stop. He apparently felt no remorse, and, at his trial, he said he took the money because he was not given the power he deserved in the organization.

I think he got just what he deserved.

*"money money money
do you feel like a pawn
in your own world?
you found the system
and you lost the pearl"*
- LAURA NYRO, "Money" 1975

*"Don't go around saying the world owes you a
living; the world owes you nothing, it was here
first."* - MARK TWAIN

• • •

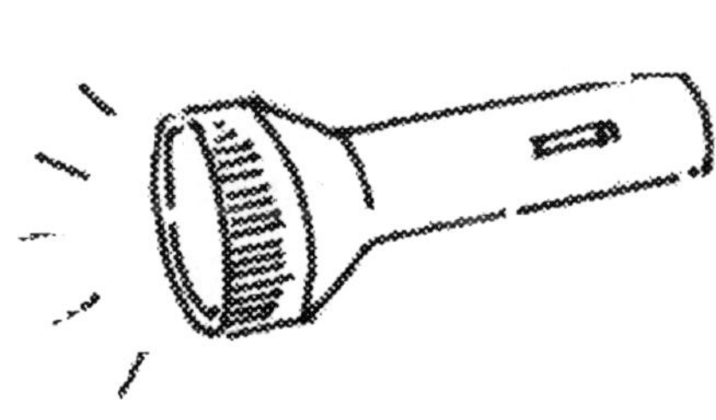

111

[58] I will always remember the day my boss absolutely "lost it" in his office. I handed him a quarterly revenue report, then sat down in the chair across from him, waiting to discuss business. He spread out the report on his desk, took one look, and went crazy. He stood up and shoved everything — and I mean *everything* — off his desk into my lap and onto the floor, all the while yelling, "I will not accept this report! It can't be right! There's no way that orders can be this low. I will not look at this until you have corrected it."

I bit my tongue and counted to ten. As we stared at each other, with all the mess laying around, he began to feel foolish. His face got a funny twisted look to it. Then I said to him, "Now, are you ready to talk about this report?" We resumed our meeting.

Sometimes I am reminded of him, usually when my toddler misbehaves.

"Remember not only to say the right thing in the
right place, but far more difficult still, to leave
unsaid the wrong thing at the tempting
moment."
- BENJAMIN FRANKLIN

"Anger has overpowered him, and driven him to
a revenge which was rather a stupid one, I must
acknowledge, but anger makes us all stupid."
- JOHANNA SPYRI, in <u>Heidi</u>

•••

[59] I am the only black woman who works in the cafeteria at a school in an upper middle class mostly white neighborhood. My new supervisor, who was on probation by the school district, had been recently transferred to our school, and I don't think she liked me from the very beginning. I minded my own business and did what she asked me to, but she yelled at me all the time. Finally I went to the manager and asked her to transfer me to another school.

The manager didn't want to transfer me because she knew I was a hard worker. She called us both in her office and asked for a description of the problems. The supervisor admitted that she had no gripe about the actual work I did, but when the manager asked her why she yelled at me, she answered, "Because she doesn't smile enough."

"The beatings will continue until morale improves." - MURPHY'S LAW

"My only concern was to get home after a hard day's work." - ROSA PARKS

•••

Index to Business Types

Do you have a bad boss story? Send it to us c/o
Bright Books, P.O. Box 50335, Austin, Texas 78763-0335

About the Authors

CARMEN DININO found the career she loves by becoming a psychotherapist, a teacher, and proud mother of Harrison. She is currently a senior staff counselor, program director, and lead grant writer for the Williamson County Council on Alcohol and Drug Abuse, and is in private practice.

GAYLE LANIER has recently launched a blissful second marriage, wherein she learned the art of angling after age 40. She comes from an entrepreneurial background and is currently a public servant. She enjoys the challenge of her pre-adolescent son, Scott.

CYNTHIA STONE loves no boss better than the one she has now, being the sole proprietor of her own marketing company. She also writes, teaches Sunday school, and walks briskly with her life-long friends and co-authors. She and her husband Gerald have a son, Jordan. She is allergic to cats.

Index to Quotes

Juanita Kreps - 99
Ring Lardner - 53
Liberace - 13
G. Gordon Liddy - 11
Abraham Lincoln - 91
Claire Boothe Luce - 38
Archibald MacLeish - 32
Groucho Marx - 55
H.L. Mencken - 9, 79
John Stuart Mill - 26
Murphy's Law - 9, 33, 115
Bob Newhart - 75
John Newton - 27
Richard Nixon - 11
Bill Nye - 55
Laura Nyro - 111
Jose Ortega y Gasset - 19
Rosa Parks - 115
Proverbs - 31, 36
Ronald Reagan - 83, 91
Burt Reynolds - 47
Bill "Bojangles" Robinson - 63
Kenny Rogers - 39
Will Rogers - 61, 69, 72
Bertrand Russell - 72
Antoine de Saint Exupéry - 24

Friends since grade school, the authors have collected wisdom and strategies gained in weekly visits together to share with those who have suffered at the hands of a bad boss.

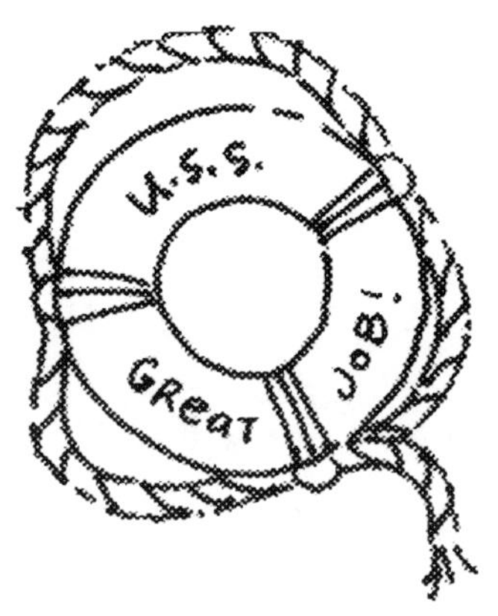

Send this postcard to any of the bosses listed - at your own risk!
Get your co-workers to buy their own books and send postcards, too.
If your boss gets plenty of feedback, maybe something good will happen.

Then again, maybe not. If your boss is as big a jerk as you think, he/she will probably collect the postcards like trophies and brag about them.

P.S. We put "Former Employee" just to protect you.

"Some things, of course, you can't change. Pretending that you have is like painting stripes on a horse and hollering 'Zebra!'"
Eddie Cantor

to:

☐ My Boss
☐ My Boss' Boss
☐ My Former Boss
☐ My Former Boss' Boss

I liked working for you (or ____________) only slightly better than...
☐ a root canal   ☐ my mother-in-law's cooking   ☐ an audit by the IRS
☐ a flat tire on the side of a hill at night in a thunderstorm

If I practiced what I learned from you (or ____________), I would...
☐ go to jail for a long, long time
☐ be slowly tortured and killed by my co-workers
☐ never draw a sober breath
☐ have trouble explaining some things to an IRS auditor

Your management style reminds me of...
☐ Mickey Mouse on a good day   ☐ a loose jackhammer
☐ Donald Duck on a bad day when he's out to get his three nephews
☐ a sledge hammer killing a fly

For your treatment of employees, you should...
☐ receive the Capt. Bligh award (remember what finally happened to him?)
☐ be booked with a one-way ticket to a war-torn third world country
☐ be hung on the wall in the employee's lounge and used for a dartboard
(frontward or backward, your choice)
☐ have to come work for me some day

The only reason I survived is because...
☐ I quit and took a better job elsewhere   ☐ you quit before you got caught
☐ you got fired just in the nick of time
☐ I got fired, but it was a blessing in disguise

Signed,

a FORMER EMPLOYEE

who is now happier and healthier !

FROM:

a former employee